T. A Griffith

Hunting Songs

T. A Griffith

Hunting Songs

ISBN/EAN: 9783744776073

Printed in Europe, USA, Canada, Australia, Japan

Cover: Foto ©Thomas Meinert / pixelio.de

More available books at **www.hansebooks.com**

Hunting Songs,

BY

T. A. GRIFFITH,

AND

OTHERS BY WELL KNOWN WRITERS.

—

LICHFIELD :

EGGINGTON AND BROWN, BIRD STREET.

1876.

CONTENTS.

PREFACE.

CANNOCK CHASE, over which the South Staffordshire Hounds now hunt so frequently, was, undoubtedly, in early times an oak forest, of great extent.

PLOT, in his County History, alludes to the derivation of Cannock or Cannock Wood, *quasi* "*Canuti Sylva.*" CANUTE having, in the time of ETHELRED, overrun most of the kingdom (Mercia being a part), in which Cannock Chase is situate.

The idea of an oak forest having existed is considerably strengthened by the fact of solitary oak trees being still extant in different parts of the Chase, *viz :*—Fair Oak, Hangman's Oak, Thieves' Oak, Coppice Oak, Lady Bromley's Oak, Warren's Oak or Teddesley Oak, and Oakedge. (?)

There is also a tradition that a squirrel could spring from oak to oak, from Hammerwich as far as Brocton (some twelve miles).

The oak fence round Wolseley Park was not, however, made from timber on the spot; as the family of WOLSELEY have now in their possession a document, signed by GENERAL FAIRFAX (soon after the temporary success of the Parliamentary forces), giving the then baronet permission to cut any quantity of oak trees in the *Forest of Needwood,* for his park pales at Wolseley, the posts of which remain, and are still quite sound.

Perhaps there may be some reason for supposing that the oak forest was gradually absorbed, the timber being used for *smelting iron*; a similar case occurring in Sussex and other parts of England, before coal was used for this purpose.

LORD HATHERTON has in his possession a most interesting Diary of the late SIR EDWARD LITTLETON, from about 1760 or 1790, recording the sport his fox hounds shewed on Cannock Chases; ome runs of extraordinary length being recorded.

At the present day, wild foxes of the old breed are occasionally found, and if the scent lies well, *hounds*, as a rule, beat *horses*, over this wild and hilly district, some parts of which are singularly picturesque.

In the spring of the year, say in the first or second week in April, if a fox is found—and hounds get away on good terms with him—the scene is well worthy of the pencil of a "GRANT."

But alas! the confines of this time honoured hunting ground are gradually, but surely, being narrowed, and probably in the next generation, coal mines will smoke in every part of it; and then no longer will be heard the cheering blast of the huntsman's horn, or the wild note of the grouse and black cock, packs of which were constantly to be seen within the last few years on most parts of this celebrated Chase.

KING EDWARD FIRST, in the eighteenth year of his reign, on the 28th May, at Westminster, granted to BISHOP

ROGER DE MEILAND (or Molend) the forest of Cannock for a free chase, which had, in more ancient times, belonged to the See of Lichfield.

In Haywood Park, which also belonged to the Bishop, were perhaps the deer, which LELAND says, the Bishop had in his manor of Shugborough, hard by, where stood the ancient mansion on the banks of the river Sowe, which was bestowed in the reign of EDWARD SIXTH, on LORD PAGET. The house was, till that time, one of the palaces of the Bishop. It is curious to note that the prelates of those days seem to have been overdone with residences, for it appears that BISHOP BOOTH, in a letter to the POPE, dated June 15th, 1448, complained that the houses attached to his See were more numerous than were necessary for use, or convenient to repair, out of the revenues of the See.

The POPE, therefore, issued a Bull, dated September, 1450, for diminishing the number of episcopal houses belonging to the See, and decreed, that the palace in Coventry, the palace in Lichfield, the castle and manor of Eccleshall, the manor of Heywode, the manor of Beaudesert, and the mansion in the Strand, near London, were sufficient for the Bishops of Coventry and Lichfield, and that they should not be obliged to build, repair, or sustain any other.

Another episcopal house of the Bishops was at Pipe, near Lichfield, although it was seldom honoured with their presence.*

In the Diocese of Hereford, about the end of the fourteenth century, the Bishop of that See appears to have

*Harwood's History of Lichfield.

iv.

maintained a hunting establishment on a grand scale as my kinsman, Mr. BASEVI SANDERS, of the "Record Office," and some time custodian of "Domesday Book" once shewed me a most interesting M.S. document, minutely describing the cost of removing his (the Bishop's) *hounds* and *horses*, to Oxfordshire or Berkshire.

In the late SQUIRE CHADWICK's time, when he hunted the South Staffordshire Country, some excellent runs were chronicled in his Journal, extracts of which have been kindly furnished to me by the present owner of *New Hall*. Two are appended.—" Wednesday, 27th December, 1826, *with my own hounds*, at Swinfen, chopped a Fox in " Freeford Pool Tail :" afterwards had a very fine hunting run from " *Brook Hay*" to near " *Twycross*," in Leicestershire."

The other run was from "Biddlesfield," in November, 1828 ; killing their Fox at "Hagley Park," after bringing him by "Shenstone," "Footherly," "Wall." "Hammerwich," "Gentleshaw," over "Beaudesert Park," by "Regent's Wood," and "Flaxley Green," close to "Rugeley Town."

Under the present management, perhaps one the best runs on record in this district, was from "New Parks," by "Langley," "New Hall," over the Birmingham and Lichfield road, into "Sutton Park," straight across it, by "Aston Coverts," on to "Aldridge," by "Forge Mills," "Biddlesfield," "The Bosses," "Footherley Rough," and "Malkin's Coppice," to "Broad Heath," by "Shenstone." This run was recorded January 26th, 1875.

T. A. G.

December 13th, 1875.

P.S.—In a notice which appeared in the *Staffordshire Advertiser* of December 11th, 1875, an account of fox hunting in Staffordshire and the adjoining Counties, during the past century, shews considerable research. Referring to the Atherstone Hunt, the writer does not come beyond MR. APPLETHWAITE'S mastership. It may therefore, perhaps, be worth recording that since his (MR. A's time) MR. C. R. COLVILE, of Lullington, MR. WILSON, formerly of Gumley, and afterwards of Leamington, CAPT. ANSTRUTHER THOMPSON, a sportsman of world-wide fame, MR. SELBY LOWNDES, of Whaddon, LORD CURZON (and for the second time CAPTAIN THOMPSON) and MR. W. E. OAKELEY, the present Master, have held this important post.

A short time since, at Thorpe Constantine, the REV. GEORGE INGE mentioned a very interesting fact (on the occasion of the presentation of his picture) *viz.* that he perfectly recollected LORD VERNON'S hounds drawing "Thorpe Gorse," he added, that in his time, sixteen Masters in succession had held the reins, but none had ever been more deservedly popular than the present one.

It will not be out of place to mention here that with LORD ANSON, and MR. APPLETHWAITE, ROBERT THURLOE, and JESSE (as huntsman and first whip), achieved an undying reputation for skill in their craft, while WILL DERRY, with MR. COLVILE, STEPHEN DICKEN, in MR. LOWNDES' time, and afterwards with MR. OAKELEY, also made their mark.

The sport shewed with MR. OAKELEY speaks for itself, as far as CASTLEMAN the present huntsman is concerned,—than vi.

whom it would be difficult to find a more determined horseman. It must not be forgotten that the late Mr. HARRY KING, the Queen's huntsman, commenced his career under R. THURLOE, in the Atherstone Country.

While on the subject of the Atherstone hunt I cannot refrain from mentioning that at Maer Hall, some years ago, the late Mr. WILLIAM DAVENPORT shewed me the hunting horn, about which, lately, a notice has appeared in the *Field* Newspaper.

The inscription on it was certainly a curious one,—stating that "with this horn, the owner, from *Tooley Brake*, hunted the first pack of fox hounds ever kept in England."

In LORD DONEGAL's time, a run from Kingsbury Wood, if I mistake not, in March, 1785, is chronicled, which in these days, is quite unparalleled. The hounds left their kennels at Fisherwick, at 6 a.m. and after drawing Bentley Park, found in Kingsbury Wood, and brought their fox across the river Tame, at Fazeley, thence by Bangley, Hints, Thickbroom, Shenstone, Stonnall, Pelsall, Bloxwich, Hilton, by the outskirts of Wolverhampton, to Penn Common, where they killed. Several horses succumbed in this memorable run, during which, of course, hounds must have changed their fox more than once or twice.

The particulars of this extraordinary day's sport are minutely described, and the canal or *navigation* (as it is termed in the account), in the neighbourhood of Wolverhampton, was crossed twice. Thus much for the Atherstone.

SIR EDWARD LITTLETON, about the same time, in his Diary, which I recollect perusing at Teddesley, in the late LORD

HATHERTON's time,—among the very many good days recorded, speaks of a great run from Teddesley to the confines of Cannock Chase, thence by Hammerwich, Muckley Corner, Wall, Swinfen, to "Lichfield Heath," where they killed their fox. The account concluding in these graphic words—"ourselves, horses and hounds tired indeed."

SIR EDWARD also mentions occasional hard runs from the Chase, over the Sowe and Trent, to Needwood Forest. One cannot but regret that the foxes of the present day have not the stoutness of those of the last century.

Having alluded briefly to the Atherstone Hunt, I cannot but add that, since 1837, on the Derbyshire borders, I have seen not a few great days in the field with the late Mr. Hugo Meynell Ingram and his father (the late squire), in whose time I well recollect meeting the celebrated actor, Mr. Young, who was a great friend, and a regular visitor at Horecross, during the hunting season. I can also well call to mind the charm of his conversation in the field.

Old Tom Leedham, the present Tom Leedham's father, was (although then an old man) a magnificent horseman, and calculated to make a lasting impression on one's mind.

At that time, and indeed for many years afterwards, the names of Mr. Trevor Yates and his brother Augustus, Mr. German Buckston, Mr. Reginald Chandos Pole, Mr. Charles Landor, Mr. E. A. and Mr. J. Holden were household words as distinguished sportsmen in the Meynell hunt, and fine riders to these far-famed hounds, while subsequently, the present Tom Leedham and his brother John were notorious as adepts in their vocation. In later times, an account (from the pen of Mr. M. T. Bass, M.P.) will suffice to shew that the wild fox in Derbyshire still exists (1870). I cannot do better than close this short notice by appending it :—

This favourite pack has had a run of sport lately, but never perhaps, since the days of the famous Hugo Meynell, great grandfather of the present spirited master, has it manifested more decisively the advantages of blood and breeding, than it displayed on Thursday last. The meet was Radborne, a synonym for good foxes and good sport, the Squire's jolly presence and cheery smile made one feel sure of a run, while an unusual field of riding men, and equipages crowded with the ladies of the county, formed a scene of animation and beauty that would be hard to match. At a quarter to twelve the bitches—what darlings ! were thrown into the Rough, and in another minute a fox was halloaed away ; he struck up the hill to the right of Hall, crossed the road through the osiers, looking towards Mickleover, where he was headed back, he recrossed the road, leaving Dalbury on his left, on to Thurvaston looking for Longford, all the way at a strong pace over a fine country, though Trusley brook brought not a few good ones to grief ; but he was again headed, and turning sharp by his right took a line back to the Rough, which, without a moment's pause, he quitted for Langley, but giving a wide berth on his right, he went straight for Cox's cover, crossed the Ashbourn road for Wild Park, by Mercaston, straight on by Kedleston Park, on his left for Markeaton gravel pit, only a long mile from Derby town ; here Tom Leedham thinks we changed, the run fox being seen crossing the road Allestree, while the fresh varmint raced up the brook course in front of Kedleston Hall, clean through the park, inclining towards Vicar wood on his left. We ran into view at Langley village, and from that point it was clear he was making for his home in the hills, alas, no more his home! his line was Mercaston, Mercaston stoop, leaving Mansel Park on the right, Bradley on the left, under Hulland, Hulland Ward to the left, crossed the Belper road and down the valley by Biggin, leaving Ideridghay on the right; forward to Blackwall house, where Tom again viewed the fox with his ladies—twenty couple, only one missing—close at his brush; but here, alas, Tom's part was done, his horse, The Knight, staggered, dropped, and died; he had carried him brilliantly, and never, in more than forty years that we have watched this gallant and judicious horseman, have we seen him ride to his hounds with more spirit, skill, and care. The hounds, however, careless of their master's troubles, still pursued their sinking game through Blackwall wood, where, despairing the shelter of his native hills, he retraced his steps down the valley for Biggin mill, and came to bay under a holly bush. Here Ringlet singly attacked him, and with Mr. Charles Eaton (a good farmer and gallant sportsman) to back her, finished one of the greatest runs we have ever seen recorded. The time was a few minutes over four hours, and the line of run exceeded thirty-two miles—the distance between extreme points was fourteen miles. The pace throughout was extraordinary for the distance, and as there were few second horsemen, it is not surprising that the party at the finish was unusually small; Sir Thomas Gresley, Mr. George Moore, jun., Mr. Charles Eaton, Miss Meynell, Hon. A. Strutt, and Mr. Bass, composed the field and sung the whoop; $7\frac{1}{2}$ couple of hounds were at the death, 9 couple were called away to a false holloa towards Atlow, and Mr. N. Curzon, Miss G. Meynell, and Mr. Travers who, till that point, had been with hounds, took them home. No one will wonder that even such men as the master, the Cokes, the two Lords Paget, W. Clowes, Willington, T. W. Evans, W. Boden, H. Evans, and many others, besides a troop of hard bitten looking strangers should have had enough in a run where four days' work was crowded in one; but the ears of the two last-named, and one or two others, caught the strains of the funeral dirge, though the sight was denied them. Tom Leedham was the hero of the day,—never man went or hunted his hounds better; he had a second horse, but as both his whips stopped at Kedleston, he had more on his hands than man could do. Sir Thomas Gresley had two horses, and both had enough of it. Mr. Bass had two, but he was nursing his second horse (Grasshopper) from the begininng, or he would never have seen the end. Sir Thomas rode his hunter home, 30 miles, and Mr. Bass rode back, more than 25. Tom declares his hounds would have done the same ground over again the next day, and we believe it. Never was pack so fast, so stout, so true!

January 31st, 1876.

PS.—An account of three most excellent runs (as far back as 1828) has just reached me, and I think them so interesting to the supporters of the present South Staffordshire pack, that I cannot refrain from having them printed. It will be seen that I am indebted to the present Squire, of New Hall, for corroborating the account copied from the *Sporting Magazine*, of 1828, by my friend, the Rev. ———, Vicar of B——n.

On Tuesday, October 14th, 1828, the "S. S. H." (Mr. H. M. Chadwick's fox hounds) had a day's sport which would have done a pack of hounds credit, even in the height of the season.

After changing foxes several times, and giving the woods a good rattling, they went away, *best pace*, with an *old* fox, from Middleton, the seat of one of the Members for War-wickshire, and had a sharp burst *up wind* for North's Wood, Moxhull Park, and Wishaw Green.

After crossing the turnpike road, they were brought, by unavoidable circumstances, to what is called a "hunting scent," but kept persevering on the line of their fox to the edge of the open commons, where the counties divide; they then turned to left, for the village of Curdworth, swam the canal, and on to-wards Dunton Wood, where they once more *got upon terms with him*, and ran in a direction for the large meadows, on the banks of the river, where reynard had waited for them among some osiers; and they ran from scent to view, and killed him in the middle of a large grass field, nearly opposite the town of Coles-hill, after a run of one hour and forty-five minutes, to the high gratification of Mr. Chadwick (who hunts his own hounds) and of a numerous field of sportsmen, among whom were some officers from the barracks, admirably mounted.

"New Hall, Jan. 29th. 1876.

"MY DEAR GRIFFITH,—Thanks very much for your letter, and also for LEGARD's, (to me) most interesting account of what I call an excellent day's sport.

"I have just looked at my father's journal, and find it

tallies with Legard's account, viz. : 'Tuesday, October, 14th, 1828, with my own hounds, cub hunting at Middleton; did not go to the woods at all; found in the small coverts, by the house. A great deal of hard running about the small coverts, and then went clean away for North's Wood and Moxhull, and on to Curdworth. Fox jumped up in view, close to the river side, in a meadow by Curdworth Bridge. Hounds ran him in view, and killed, in middle of a grass field, near Coleshill. Very good run. Rode 'Earwig' (a two-year old fox) I, all night from Birmingham to London.'

" ' Monday, October 27th, 1828, with my own hounds. First day of regular hunting at Watford Gap; found in Sutton Park, a long hunting run, and killed in the meadows, opposite Birmingham, Aston Church. Two hours and twenty-five minutes. Rode ' Maria.' '

" ' Friday, November 21st, 1828, with my own hounds, at Packwood; found in Arnold's Wood; a very severe run, and much of it very straight and fast, by Beoly, Studley, Colton Park, Sir C. Throckmorton's, to a wood of Lord Hertford's, three miles from Alcester, and were beat. I was capitally carried. My grey horse 'Contribution' died on his way home, from the severity of the run. ' Jem ' rode him. Mr. Holyoak lent Tom a horse towards the end. I rode ' Earwig ' and ' Mystery.' ' I have sent you an account of two days' good sport, copied from my father's journal, of same year, which I think may amuse you.

" J. D. C."

SOUTH STAFFORDSHIRE

HUNTING SONG.

1875.

Air, " *John Peel.*"

D'ye ken Captain Browne, the master of our pack ?
D'ye ken him with his hounds upon his hunter's back ?
When *Damager* and *Dowager* that couple fleet and crack,
Are racing for the lead in the morning.

(Chorus.)
    For the sound of the horn for me has a grace,
    And the cry of the hounds, when at their best pace ;
    For who would not rise to go hunting on Cank Chase ?
    With the South Stafford hounds in the morning.

D'ye ken the Lord of Teddesley, Baron Hatherton by name ?
D'ye ken a fox at Pottall is sure to be at home ?
'Tis superfluous to add, he's on the roll of fame,
As our stanchest preserver in the morning.
    For the sound of the horn, &c.

D'ye ken the Baron's Sons distinguished horsemen are?
The Colonel, the Commander, the astute Counsellor;
Mr. Henry the Colonist, also a sportsman rare,
One who'll vie for the brush in the morning.
    For the sound of the horn, &c.

D'ye ken how great our obligations are
To the noble Lord that owns the charming " Beaudesert?"
And but for Mr. Darling, 'tis true that we should fare
But poorly on Cank Chase in the morning.
    For the sound of the horn, &c.

D'ye ken that Robert Wyatt, a sportsman keen and good
Should induce the Lord of Shugbro'? to subscribe if he would
Represent the matter fairly, then probably we should
Be sure to find a fox in the morning.
    For the sound of the horn, &c.

D'ye ken Sir Charles Clifford from Hatherton Hall?
D'ye ken his sons and daughter, the fairest of them all?
For at Shoal Hill, Fullmoor, or Mansty Wood, we shall
Hope to find a fox in the morning.
    For the sound of the horn, &c.

D'ye ken the gallant Colonel, residing at Freeford?
Were I but in his stockings, I assure you on my word
I'd keep a stud of hunters, who, if they could not ford,
Should jump a river when a hunting in the morning.
    For the sound of the horn, &c.

D'ye ken at Wolseley, that Baronet whose name
Already has achieved a character for fame?
And will, as a horseman, surely put to shame
Many sportsmen, who go hunting in the morning.
    For the sound of the horn, &c.

D'ye ken Squire Chadwick with his joyous beaming face?
On *Helter*, a hunter, once famous in a race;
Charles Forster, and his brother Frank, racing for a place,
Both authorities! on hunting in the morning.
    For the sound of the horn, &c.

D'ye ken Squire Barclay of Middleton Hall
Is a specimen good, an example for all?
For there is no fear of fences or dread of a fall,
If we find at Trickley Coppice in the morning.
    For the sound of the horn, &c.

The Squires of Swinfen, Hints, Canwell, Hopwas Hays,
Possess fine coverts much entitled to our praise;
And most sincerely, our voices we will raise
To thank them for our hunting in the morning.
    For the sound of the horn, &c.

D'ye ken the great Ale Kings of Burton-upon-Trent,
Are notable sportsmen, and support have always lent?
In subscribing many " ponies " which yearly have been sent
For the aid of our hounds in the morning.
    For the sound of the horn, &c.

D'ye ken Squire Manley's always to the fore?
On *Whalebone* a hunting celebrity of yore,
In A. G.'s possession, many great runs could he score,
With the Meynell hounds, and others in the morning.
    For the sound of the horn, &c.

D'ye ken Squire Lane sufficiently has prov'd,
Tho' no longer a horseman the science well he's lov'd?
For full many a mile a sportsman must have rov'd
To find more holding coverts in the morning.
    For the sound of the horn, &c.

D'ye ken Squire Calthorpe erst at Melton good?
With a string of flying hunters cleverly that could
Clear in their stride the " Whissendine's " famed flood,
When hunting with the Quorn hounds in the morning.
    For the sound of the horn, &c.

D'ye ken Squire Tredwell on *Rhoderick Dhu*?
D'ye ken how he rides when the fox is in full view;
With the " General " from Pipe, and Harry Martin too,
When hounds are running hard in the morning.
    For the sound of the horn, &c.

D'ye ken Squire Chance at Four Oaks is a friend
Who deserves recognition for the aid that he will lend?
For the South Stafford hounds, I myself do apprehend
Have no steadier supporter in the morning.
    For the sound of the horn, &c.

D'ye ken young Squire Fox on a galloping good brown ?
How heartily he thrusts him along the breezy down,
For one day, with Griffith mounted, he seems almost to have
O'er the wilds of Cannock Chase in the morning.   [flown
 For the sound of the horn, &c.

D'ye ken a horseman tall; with his silvery white hair ?
D'ye ken that he is mounted on a famous bay mare ?
D'ye ken when the fox is rous'd from his lair ?
How he'll ride to the hounds in the morning.
 For the sound of the horn, &c.

D'ye ken Sir Robert's coverts ? that if a south-east wind
Is blowing towards Hints, in a twinkling we shall find
A fox, and get away, at a pace quite to my mind,
From the Gorse at " Drayton Manor ", in the morning.
 For the sound of the horn, &c.

D'ye ken Mr. Jervis, how keen he is for sport ?
He has youth upon his side, and is of the right sort ;
While his neighbour Mr. Bagnall proves that hunting is his forte
With the South Stafford hounds in the morning.
 For the sound of the horn, &c.

D'ye ken Arthur Perks and his brother John yclept
*The " Baron ? " (immortalised in verse) these men have leapt
When young, such rasping fences, now never kept
In these degenerate days when a hunting.
 For the sound of the horn, &c.

D'ye ken as fine a sportsman as ever followed hounds,
" Frank Yates of Barr ? " I'll lay a hundred pounds,
When by the coverts side the loud view holloa sounds,
My friend's amongst the first flight in the morning.
    For the sound of the horn, &c.

Squire Mott of Wall, and Mr. Seargeant at the Bank,
The former good for ten, the latter free and frank ;
Would be very much concerned did they hear that a blank
Had occur'd while out a hunting in the morning.
    For the sound of the horn, &c.

D'ye ken Mr. Coath, and George Strongy on his black ?
D'ye ken that both horsemen are close upon the pack ?
D'ye ken 'tis true, of courage there's no lack ?
When these sportsmen come to ride in the morning.
    For the sound of the horn, &c.

D'ye ken Mr. Graham famous for his stud
At Yardley ? where you'll find the very essence of pure blood ;
Mrs. Graham, all admit to be a pattern fine and good,
To be admir'd out a hunting in the morning.
    For the sound of the horn, &c.

D'ye ken Bernard Gilpin, Mrs. Gilpin, Master " Will ? "
Always mounted on good quality, apparently that will
Make a name over hurdles, win a race without a spill,
If they stand upon their legs in the morning.
    For the sound of the horn, &c.

D'ye ken that noted steeple chaser, *Hall Court* by name ?
A steed that has on Aintree Course achiev'd a niche in fame ;
How easily could he defeat (even were he lame)
Most hunters that are ridden in the morning.
    For the sound of the horn, &c.

D'ye ken that Lawyer Glover, of Cannock has a lair
Either for a dog-fox, or vixen ? (p'raps the pair)
At Huntingdon ; a covert, where there always is a fair
Prospect of good sport in the morning.
    For the sound of the horn, &c.

The Thomas's of Bloxwich, and Stanley of that place,
Are all well mounted horsemen, who boldly go the pace
On a good scenting day ; when hounds can fairly race
Unchecked, and kill their fox in the morning.
    For the sound of the horn, &c.

D'ye ken Squire Bagot and Thomas Pickernill ?
D'ye ken how they ride regardless of a spill ?
Osborne, winner of the Leger ! and Skelton who shall fill
The stave, to make my rhyme up, in the morning.
    For the sound of the horn, &c.

D'ye ken Joseph Sankey fam'd for horses rare ?
Either for the hunting field, or driving in a pair ;
And I'll venture even money, he's at Ballinasloe fair,
Finding steeds to go a hunting in the morning.
    For the sound of the horn, &c.

Percy Burnett well attired, neatly mounted on a bay,
Is here despite th' attaction of the Meynell hounds to-day ;
Mrs. Burnett and her sister, with their equipage so gay,
Also grace our hunting pageant of this morning.
    For the sound of the horn, &c.

Messrs. Madeley and Kynock, both are sportsmen keen,
But unluckily for us, they are but seldom seen ;
Repitition of ill-luck does but excite their spleen,
When with us they come a hunting in the morning.
    For the sound of the horn, &c.

D'ye ken any gentlemen at Coffee housing great ?
Who will jabber and jaw about hunting in much state ;
But who'll shirk every fence, and open every gate,
Whenever he goes hunting in the morning.
    For the sound of the horn, &c.

D'ye ken Mr. Trevor of the " Swan," Mr. Bown,
A. Morgan, and his daughter too, and many in the town
Of Lichfield ? for sporting proclivities well known,
Always ready to go hunting in the morning.
    For the sound of the horn, &c.

Dy'e ken Ralph Sadler, a promising light weight
And grandson to a sportsman ? in his day a very great
†Performer with the "Atherstone," when many and many a gate
He delighted in jumping in the morning.
    For the sound of the horn, &c.

D'ye ken that Berkeley Paget single handed has laid low
A grisly-bear (near Denver) and a shaggy buffalo,
And on the hills of Derbyshire, all riding men well know
His daring feats of horsemanship when hunting.
    For the sound of the horn, &c.

D'ye ken Justice James, John Brown of the Grange,
Captain Webster, Captain Tongue, Mr. Owen who'll arrange
To mount any sportsman, who comes within the range,
For a reasonable guerdon in the morning.
    For the sound of the horn, &c.

D'ye ken Jack Boore, our kennel huntsman neat?
D'ye ken Jack Boore, how workmanlike his seat?
D'ye ken how he rides to the leading hounds so fleet?
If there is but a scent in the morning.
    For the sound of the horn, &c.

See Jackson, Kendrick, Grammar, Bennell, eager for a start,
From the covert side at Middleton each vowing in his heart;
Neither Kempson, William White, or Smith, as yet have learnt
Of giving them the go-by in the morning.   [the art
    For the sound of the horn, &c.

William Dester, a famed rider who resides at Seckington,
A more consummate horseman, or bolder ne'er was known;
The formidable obstacles, that in his day he's flown,
Would be a caution to most men in the morning!
    For the sound of the horn, &c.

B

Jack Prinsep and his brother Will are sportsmen of an age,
Coeval with ‡ " Bob Thurlow " whose fame upon the page
Of history will flourish, as a " Huntsman " erst the rage,
For jumping gates after hounds in the morning.
    For the sound of the horn, &c.

D'ye ken amongst the flying best performers in the field,
Most ladies in the saddle must to Miss A. Cowpland yield?
But for knowledge of the science you must travel far a field,
To surpass the Master's lady in the morning.
    For the sound of the horn, &c.

Walter Landor from Lee Hall, and Mr. Smith who hails
From Curbro' with his daughter, have shown that no rails
Are too formidable, or strong ; nor jagged park pales,
Can daunt them when a hunting in the morning.
    For the sound of the horn, &c.

Messrs. Marsh, Barrah, Bawcutt, Hatton, Mynors, Orton, Peake,
John Gardner, and his brother James, all willingly will speak
Seriously at home, or when out upon a freak,
In praise of our hounds in the morning.
    For the sound of the horn, &c.

D'ye ken Mr. Foden, well mounted on a blood?
Full of quality and mettle, who looks as if he stood
For the Liverpool Grand National a fair chance and a good,
Provided he stands training in the morning.
    For the sound of the horn, &c.

Squire Barker of Beacon House, mounted on a mare
That looks like going, and of quality rare,
Jacob Stordy, Mr. Cooper, and Messrs. Barnes (the pair),
All are here on this fine hunting morning.
     For the sound of the horn, &c.

Mr. Pierman Smith, and his son from Walsall Town,
Mr. Williams, Mr. Ellis, Mr. Parrish, Mr. Brown ;
Each of these sportsmen an example good have shewn,
To make their friends come hunting in the morning.
     For the sound of the horn, &c,

Mr. Negus of Lynn Lane with his fair wife at his side,
Does but seldom grace the meet at the gorse or woodland side ;
Still gratified all would be to see this couple ride,
A hunting with our hounds in the morning.
     For the sound of the horn, &c.

Squire Davies of Footherley, in Oxfordshire is known,
As a sportsman of mark from his heel to his crown ;
No steed that he rides, was e'er seen to be blown,
Or distress'd, with the hounds in the morning.
     For the sound of the horn, &c.

The General from Pipe, ye ken himself has shewn,
Thoroughly a sportsman to his very back bone ;
A glutton for the craft and invariably prone,
To see what fun he can in the morning.
     For the sound of the horn, &c.

Mr. Clements of the " Midland " has a celebrated house,
Admirably adapted for a bridegroom and his spouse ;
Who, on their wedding tour, would with difficulty rouse
Themselves from balmy slumbers in the morning.
    For the sound of the horn, &c.

The Leedhams of Hoar Cross, ye ken they are a race
Of distinguish'd fine huntsmen who've justly earn'd a place,
In the memory of all who've seen them go the pace,
From Radbourn's famous covert in the morning.
    For the sound of the horn, &c.

D'ye ken Tom Leedham's sire ? some forty years ago,
Was invincible on Cannock Chase, as sure as hounds could go,
From Beaudesert to Shugboro', the pace was never slow
When Joe and Tom were whippers-in that morning.
    For the sound of the horn, &c.

And now I have recounted my num'rous hunting friends,
Who have figured as good sportsman o'er a period that extends
Full forty years, or more alas ! a warning note it sends,
Since Dick Brown and I first hunted in the morning.
    For the sound of the horn, &c.

For we've followed our master o'er gate, stile, and bar,
Thro' the black thorn fence from Hopwas up to Barr ;
From Black Slough, New Parks and Cannock Chase afar,
When hounds can press their fox in the morning.
    For the sound of the horn, &c.

Then fill to John Browne a bowl, nay fill
A bumper in his praise, nor a drop ever spill;
For a sportsman like him we trust we may still
Retain to hunt the hounds in the morning.
    For the sound of the horn, &c.

HUNTING SONG,

1872.

Air, " Batchelor's Hall."

The first of November once more has come round,
That season enchanting! again the sweet sound
Of the horn, to all Fox-hunting Sportsmen so dear
Suggests to us sport, horses, hounds, and good cheer.
See our master Lord Henry on *Barmaid,* a grey,
That to every appearance can show us the way.

> Hark away ! hark away ! all nature seems gay,
> And Aurora with smiles ushers in the bright day.

His Lordship we're delighted to see again sound,
From his fracture last year when he was hurl'd to the ground ;
His appointments are perfect, and as to his seat,
There can be no cavil or doubt about that ;
As master, his temper severely is tried,
When " Gents " so persistently his hounds over-ride.

> Hark away ! &c.

The Marquis of Anglesey's first on the list,
A more princely subscriber there does not exist ;
To Sir Thomas his tenant, our best thanks are due,
For a fine lot of Foxes can Beaudesert show.
Squire Spode, Col. Sullivan, Shugborough's Lord,
All have fine coverts, which good sport afford.

    Hark away ! &c.

Charles Wolseley of Wolseley rides on a grey mare,
You can't easily match, her condition is rare ;
Well bred is Sir Charles with blue blood in his vein,
Which dates further back than the Conqueror's reign.
Squire Manley on *Whalebone*, away he goes clean !
And 'twill take all your time if to catch him you mean.

    Hark away ! &c.

Squire Chadwick is here always genial and hearty,
Should he be away incomplete is our party,
His taste in apparel undeniably good,
A more popular sportsman in stockings ne'er stood ;
Old estates has at Rochdale, at Ridware, New Hall,
His ancestor " Mavesyn " at Shrewsbury did fall.

    Hark away ! &c.

Littleton, Walferstan, Corbett, each name
On history's page, full well known to fame,
In the counties of Staffordshire, Warwickshire, Salop,

These noble and gentlemen know how to gallop.
Much indebted we must be to Hatherton's Lord.
For the sport that the coverts of Teddesley afford.

     Hark away ! &c.

Sir Clifford of Elmhurst, and with him his son,
Right glad we're to see them the scarlet put on ;
Well they support us with money and care
Of the Gorse, Vicars' Coppice, Tom Hay, and elsewhere.
The Prince of good fellows, Fred Wombwell, whose jokes,
Would e'en from a hermit a smile almost coax.

     Hark away ! &c.

Shrewsbury and Talbot that popular Earl,
Has 'mongst Old English mansions a genuine pearl
In beautiful Ingestre, but Foxes, alas !
Has none, though coverts are fine and country all grass ;
But his Lordship, we hear, some fresh keepers has got,
And sincerely, we hope, a more favourable lot.

     Hark away ! &c.

Colonel Dyott for Lichfield the gallant M.P.,
Good for a couple of " ponies " is he ;
His neighbour, Squire Broun, comes not out with the hounds,
But well aids our coffers by giving ten pounds.
Squire Lane of King's Bromley, whose support is so good
For such coverts as Black Slough and Ravenshaw Wood.

     Hark away ! &c.

Dandy, Berkeley, and Legard, so jovial to meet,
That to see them with hounds is indeed a great treat,
All mounted on nags with a fine turn of speed,
What a rattle they go! these fine horsemen indeed ;
When hounds find a fox, out of covert they dash
At a pace quite alarming, through the fences they crash.

    Hark away! &c.

Squire Floyer of Hints, must not by the rood
Be omitted, as once he was wonderfully good
As a Sportsman, in Applethwaite's time would he go
O'er the country and fences as straight as a crow.
The Canwell Estate we hear by report,
Into hands has just passed, that we trust will show sport.

    Hark away! &c.

Teddy Ley, from the old Roman Village of Wall,
Hard rider is he, with no fear of a fall ;
Cis Stephens, George Maidstone, 'clept galloping " George,"
Is as mustard as keen, right ahead will he forge ;
Beale, Arnold, Peal, Hammond, these artists all vie,
In producing such boots, leather breeches, and tie.

    Hark away! &c.

See here comes Bob Levett, the Packington Squire,
Your manners now mind, else the fat's in the fire ;
But at Hopwas he always can find us a litter,

c

When in coverts hard by our time we oft fritter ;
His brother Squire John, too, though seldom he's out,
Is good for a " tenner," each season throughout.

> Hark away ! &c.

Squire Bagnall, of Shenstone, at Footherley brake,
Has a lair for a Fox, whence should he but take
To the cover Cock Heath, or far-fam'd Biddlesfield,
Quite sure to get down are some of the field ;
For blind is the country, the banks too are rotten,
And this is a fact which must not be forgotten.

> Hark away ! &c.

Charles Forster of Lysways, keen sportsman and true,
Though rolling in money, is content with a screw.
Frank Forster, his brother, whose nom de plume's " Fors "
Already an M. H., and well skilled in the laws ;
He looks well as a Counsel in wig and in gown,
But still loves the country much more than the town.

> Hark away ! &c.

But here comes a Soldier and Captain so bold,
With meerschaum in mouth, as the morning is cold,
In military tactics undoubtedly great,
For deep authors he studies both early and late ;
While on " Gwyllym " the herald (whom some think a bore)
Profound his research is and learned his lore.

> Hark away ! &c.

Who's this horseman so tall and so keen for a start ?
Quite grey on the head, who can still take his part ;
Though for thirty-eight seasons this country he's known,
Where there's scarcely a fence o'er which he's not flown ;
He's still young at heart, and not bound to be last,
On the day he likes best, when hounds really go fast.

    Hark away ! &c.

Here's a horseman all over, Will Tredwell by name,
From Eastfields he hails, and is well known to fame ;
His steeds *Warrior*, *Bentinck*, *Bismark*, and *Kildare*,
All weight-carrying hunters and specimens rare ;
For if there's a scent, and we're in for a burst,
On either of these he is bound to be first.

    Hark away ! &c.

But hold ! here's a lady quite matchless in frame,
And who should she be, but Squire Chadwick's fair dame ;
What hands ! seat ! and figure ! how graceful her mien,
A long way you'll go, 'ere her equal is seen ;
Whether seated in saddle, or at lunch at New Hall,
She's a word of kind welcome for one and for all.

    Hark away ! &c.

With his Sons all well mounted, see the Amington Squire,
How superbly he's horsed, and what perfect attire ;
With his neighbour, Frank Willington, who let us hope,

Will for many years yet, with much younger men cope,
In crossing the country, on horses so good,
Fine movers he rides, and all of pure blood.

  Hark away! &c.

Barclay, Madeley, and Pemberton, stanch men and true,
Would please us much more, did their faces they shew
More frequently, still we much prize their support
In maintaining in Staffordshire Fox-hunting Sport;
Men good in position, with pockets well lined,
Such as these, sooth to say, we are anxious to find.

  Hark away! &c.

Frank James of Aldridge, and Frank Yates of Barr,
Exceeding good fellows and sportsmen they are,
For when the hunt's over and homeward we hie,
The savoury sirloin and well-flavoured pork pie
Are graciously offered to all that are here,
Be their choice what it may, Liqueurs, Sherry, or Beer.

  Hark away! &c.

Here's Gilpin on *Colonist*, one that can race,
And when he's intended can go a great pace ;
Will's sire learnt his craft on famed Hednesford's hill side,
When John and George Hawkes knew well how to ride ;
Mrs. Gilpin, Will's Stepdam, oft graces our meet,
With the hounds at " Four Crosses," on old Watling Street.

  Hark away! &c.

One other fair ladye and then my theme's done,
It is Miss Alice Cowpland, A 1 in a run ;
So firm is her seat, that no horse old or young,
Can of her get much change when her nerve is well strung ;
The fences look small, and if hounds make a pace,
Few ladies there are can beat her in the race.

    Hark away ! &c.

Walter Boden, of Derby, among riders a crack,
Does not often come out with our Staffordshire Pack.
Paget Mosley Antinous self, in good look,
'Twere a sin to omit from the page of this book ;
Quite faultless his figure, how well made his clothes,
His button-hole daintily decked with a rose.

    Hark away ! &c.

But one noted Sportsman, alas ! is not here,
The General from "Pipe," to all of us dear ;
Sincerely we trust, that 'ere long he'll return,
And show us the way as of yore in a run ;
For go where you will, among genial good hearts,
One more honest and true does not beat in these parts.

    Hark away ! &c.

The Grahams of Yardley, of world-wide repute,
Both welters to look at, and more than six foot.
George Brian from Ireland, a man of renown,

A horseman superb from his heel to his crown.
Tom Pickenill, an artist, atop of the tree,
As witness his triumphs on the course of Aintree.

    Hark away ! &c.

Squire Davis of Footherley, a yeoman so bold,
Bad taste it would be to leave out in the cold.
From the neighbouring town, the Coldfield of Sutton,
Dr. Smith and Ben Long (so famed for his mutton),
And the Dr.'s fair lady, so nicely appointed,
How well does she grace the steed she has mounted.

    Hark away ! &c.

Those noted good sportsmen, the Turners of Brum,
Of the Warwickshire country are fond of the cream ;
Well can they judge the sham sportsmen from real,
Keen hands they are, and from this there's no appeal.
Several other supporters both here and elsewhere,
Must excuse us should haply their names not appear.

    Hark away ! &c.

The next on my list is my friend Mr. White,
Who for years past, in black, rode among the first flight ;
But now he's donn'd scarlet ; had I but his coin,
A similar garb, I myself would put on.
John Brown, of the Grange, looking sound as a bell,
Owen, Host of the " George," a sportsman rides well.

    Hark away ! &c.

Harry Martin well known on the wilds of Cank Wood,
As a bad one to beat by field or by flood.
Stordy of Swinfen and Cooper the Vet,
Cheatle who'll give his friends plenty of wet,
Kendrick of Weeford in boots and black cap,
Stanley from Bloxwich, how he scorns a gap.

    Hark away ! &c.

But here's a mistake! George Strongie's not here,
How is this? with a sportsman a stranger to fear,
A horseman so neat, and of pace such a judge,
I only can hope he's not taken the pledge,
For in Tom Chawner's day, that old sportsman so rare !
Master George was a keen hand at hunting the hare.

    Hark away ! &c.

Here's Jim Hand of Shirrall, whose help-mate so dear,
Is the theme of all sportsmen for giving good cheer,
For when Trickley and New Parks have each held a fox,
Straight there we make off or to Jackson's snug box ;
James Dean too of Brereton, and Landor who came,
From the stock of Charles Landor that sportsman of fame.

    Hark away ! &c.

Tom Blurton of Hammerwich, known as a shot,
At Pigeons, Grouse, Partridges, Pheasants, what not ?
Is here on his mare and can lead you a dance,

Such a pace does she go! she can gallop and prance!
Her fences she flies, and she's sure to get through,
For she is quick as a cat, and quite cunning too.
    Hark away! &c.

The M.P.'s who support us, Bass, Hardy, M'Clean,
Those for East Stafford and Derby are keen.
Major Thorney, Squires Chance, Vaughan, Jervis, and Tongue,
Not by any means least are these in the throng.
The two Captains Peel, so upright in their seat,
In the saddle they're sportsmen not easily beat.
    Hark away! &c.

His worship Mayor Symonds, Squires Seckham and Gretton,
J. V. Hall, Ratcliff, Elkington, men of distinction,
Kempson, John Barnes, Lakin, Sankey and Gillman,
Rollason, Eggington, Crosskey, A. Morgan,
Squire Garnett, two Palmers, Mann, Roberts, and Trevor,
All these gentlemen say "Fox-hunting for ever."
    Hark away! &c.

Minors, Marsh, Proffitt, Elwell, Bown, Dorsett, and Taylor,
Seargeant, Coath, Averill, and Captain Shaw Hellier,
Mr. Wayte, Mr. Fell, Lawyer Clarke, and Judge Spooner,
Peake, Mills, and Gardner, Will Smith and his brother;
Come out then do honor to this far famed pack,
And if hunters you have none, why then come on a hack.
    Hark away! &c.

Winterton's coverts at Alrewas Hayes,
We surely must mention in accents of praise,
While the neighbouring wood, the famous Brook Hay,
Safe in the hands of Charles Crisp is to day.
A great run was from hence with full many a fall,
In Lord Lichfield's to day, to Earl Howe's at Gopsall.

    Hark away ! &c.

Langley Gorse, that famed covert was made by the Baron
Webster, whose equal we rarely now look on,
That keenest of sportsmen ! most excellent fellow ! .
'Twould have done your heart good to have heard his view holloa !
Mr. Horsfall now reigns, vice Webster deceased,
And should we but find there, why right well we are pleased.

    Hark away ! &c.

Nash and Charles Keeling, and Rodgers so smart,
True sportsmen and eager to get a good start.
Charles Stubbs too ! that horseman who always is wont,
If e'er there's a scent to go right to the front.
These gentlemen only come out on Cank Chase,
Notwithstanding we're right glad to welcome their face.

    Hark away ! &c.

Here's Bob Wyatt of Acton, though not a subscriber,
I'll give him a stanza by way of reminder ;
He is fond of the sport, though fonder is he,

D

As stroke of an Eight-oar on river to be ;
On Cam and on Thames, he's led many a race,
But now he's betaken himself to the Chase.

     Hark away ! &c.

Now Gentles you'll say I have written enough,
To tire your patience if not make you cough ;
Every Swell I've recounted the country throughout,
Stay ! Bagot of Pipe must not be left out,
A lover of sport, Winter, Summer, and Spring,
He is good for a pony, and that's the right thing.

     Hark away ! Hark away ! while our spirits are gay,
     Let us drink to the joys of the next coming day.

SOUTH STAFFORDSHIRE
HUNTING SONG,

1870.

Here's St. Valentine's Day and the snow's on the ground,
　　And the turf and the plough the ice locks,
With nags in condition, and hounds fit to go,
　　We ought to be hunting the fox.

What prettier sight on a fine hunting morn
　　Than to see this crack pack now in vogue,
Will Wilson on *Chatterbox*, Joe on *the Cob*,
　　And His Lordship on *Arrah-na-Pogue*.

Here's Chadwick so genial and hearty,
　　And the General riding *Bo-Peep*,
And the Reverend Vicar of B———n,
　　For whom nothing's too wide or too deep.

Here's Dandy bestriding *Augusta*,
    And Berkeley returned from the west,
And I guess no New York filibuster
    Of His Lordship could e'er get the best.

Hark to *Gambler*, holloas Lord Henry,
    Elenn in there, *Drayman*, *Old Man.*
Tally-ho, screeches Joe, at the woods lower end,
    Hark holloa, the fun has begun.

Crash! out of the covert comes Griffith
    And dashes away as he's wont,
At the tail of the hounds always handy,
    He means to stick well to the front.

Whence comes this preposterous funker
    A-Macadamizing like fun,
Who'll swear to each credulous younker,
    He, himself, had the best of the run.

Upwind forty minutes, they race him,
    When, who-hoop, ends this gallop so fine,
And Lord Henry, the pink of politeness,
    Gives the Brush, to my fair VALENTINE.

SOUTH STAFFORDSHIRE

HUNTING SONG,

1868.

Air, " *The Cork Leg.*"

I sing of the glorious South Staffordshire pack,
Of Lord Henry, who hunts his establishment crack;
And his field between whom, there's of concord no lack,
For they swear by the lord, and he swears at them back.
    Ritooral looral loo, &c.

At each gay button tickler, whenever he's crossed,
He'll swear like the deuce, never heeding the cost;
But when he swears most, is whenever there's frost,
Singing " Perdidi diem " this day I have lost!
    Ritooral, &c.

There's General Phillips the honorary sec.,
He'll go while they're running, at risk of his neck;
But though little of ditches or doubles he'll reck,
He's often been heard to pray hard for a check (cheque).
    Ritooral, &c.

There's Griffith a bruiser, a devil to rush,
A young un in heart, though he's long in the tush;
In covert or out, will his tongue never hush,
But when the fox goes, there he's close to the brush.
    Ritooral, &c.

The next one that comes, is the sporting J. C.,
Wherever hounds go, there he's eager to be;
But he's fond of conversing and societee,
So remarkably frequently " herded " is he.
    Ritooral, &c.

There's Wilson, now stranger, be careful that you
Aint free with your tongue, for he's free with his too;
He'll gallop like blazes, and shout and halloa
Dont holloa you fool! till you're sure of a view!
    Ritooral, &c.

Of opinions a difference perhaps there may be,
Of the fox-viewing powers of Mr. E. Ley;
But this I can tell you, betwixt you and me,
In his flask, he has something much stronger than tea.
    Ritooral, &c.

See! See! there he goes! thro' the country he shoots,
Bestriding the whitest and wildest of brutes;
'Tis Milney—how wondrous the cut of his boots,
His resplendent new pink, and his breeches from Toots.
    Ritooral, &c.

See covered with mud from the head to his heel,
Comes Charley, delighted at murdering Peel,
Or fresh from Hand's luncheon and flushed with the meal,
Endeavouring Smith's favourite hunters to steal.
  Ritooral, &c.

There's Willington too, with his pencil he's great,
And at taking off heads, he's really first-rate,
Still once drawing covert, he drew off so late,
That he ne'er even saw them take off Reynard's pate.
  Ritooral, &c.

There's the Ladies, God bless them wherever they may be!
Yet some say they're better at home at their tea;
For 'tis painful to witness, and fearsome to see,
Lovely woman when cutting a voluntaree.
  Ritooral, &c.

There's Cheatle, Jackson, and Co., a true sportsman like band,
Good fox-hunting farmers, the best in the land,
They'll liquor you up, till you barely can stand,
Till the field gets quite heady and quite out of hand.
  Ritooral, &c.

Here's long life to the hunt! may it e'er find the knack,
Of pressing well forward and never hark back;
May it ne'er find of friends or of foxes a lack,
So pay up your subscriptions, and drink to the pack.
  Ritooral, &c.

SOUTH STAFFORDSHIRE

HUNTING SONG,

1868.

—   —

" The Bought Brush, or the Bottle-washer Belaboured."

It was a Bottle-washer, and he wished to have a treat,
So he took on hire a quadruped and trotted to the meet,
Would you know the hounds and country where he went to have
    his lark ?
The hounds were Henry Paget's, and the meet was Sutton Park.

Well! the meet was very crowded—Sutton teemed with man
    and horse,
For the riding sportsmen mustered in the most tremendous force ;
And our friend among their party cut a devil of a shine,
(He was very much respected in the bottle-washing line).

But alas! sad mutability! how soon their spirits sank,
When gorse on gorse, and copse on copse, were all of them
    drawn blank ;
Those Brummagems so late elate, so game for lark and fun,
They couldn't find a fox, and so they couldn't have a run.

Men's hearts were sore and sulky in the hunting field that day,
J. C. was praying loudly, as J. C. knows how to pray ;
The sporting gents from Brummagem were cursing to a man,
And Lord Henry muttered "d——n," as only British nobles can.

But suddenly, midst all these sounds of murmurings and woe,
A joyous cry is heard aloud, the stirring "Tally ho!"
Each hard and wellknown rider bold with ecstasy goes mad,
And throws his penny Pickwick down, and hustles up his Prad.

But, oh! too short that Fox's life, no run could there be had,
Full soon the sportsmen swore again, full soon they cursed like
    mad ;
And told—in language which to write—my sense of duty
    shocks,
How an eager would-be Sutton sportsman killed the wily fox.

Oh! slowly, and oh! solemnly, the party gathered round,
Where the body of their victim lay extended on the ground ;
When suddenly a voice is heard, which cries "good gracious
    lads,
Why, who the devil's got his pate, and where's his brush and
    pads ?"

Oh! great was the amazement, and the questioning began,
When from out the crowd of jabberers stepped out a Sutton
    man,—
Says he, "that Bottle-washing cove, I know, has got the brush,
He paid two-bob and took the tail, and hooked it with a rush."

E

"Which way?" exclaims the Master, and "Which way?" ex-
    claim the Whips,
The crowd of bold pedestrians were ready with their tips—
"Lay on the Hounds, ye devils, come along, my jovial cocks,
We'll hunt the Bottle-washer, if we cannot hunt the fox."

"*Ranter*" hits "the Bottle-washer" off, in manner very fine,
"*Young Frolic*" and "*Old Melody*" are soon upon his line;
See, see them, how they flash along, all racing like the wind,
For the bloated Bottle-washer leaves a burning scent behind.

The Hounds give tongue—heads up, sterns down—the field is
    mad with glee,
But that Bottle-washer's agony was terrible to see;—
They race him over hill and dale, they chase him thro' the plain,
He'd have given fifty pounds to be in Brummagem again.

But still they do not gain on him—he yet may be in luck;
But no! the worthy Rector's Son emerges from the ruck!
He gains upon his victim—overhauls him, hand o'er hand,
Till he heads the Bottle-washer back, and brings him to a stand.

The way he cursed and rated him—it passes all belief;—
"You stole the brush! you know you did, you Bottle-washing
    thief;"
Then he upped his whip, and beat him on the head, and sides,
    and back,
And he beat the Bottle-washer, till he beat him blue and
    black.

Oh! the Bottle-washer whimpered, and the Bottle-washer
   sighed,
And the Bottle-washer blubbered, and the Bottle-washer cried ;
Bold B—df—rd beat him, while ye yelled—" Give up the brush,
   you fool !"
While Lord Henry holloed—" Serve him right, but duck him
   in the pool !"

Bold B—df—rd's name shall flourish, and the tale shall never
   hush,
How he beat the Bottle-washer who skedaddled with the brush;
And the children of his children shall tell how he made his
   mark,
How he beat the Brum brush-prigger up and down through
   Sutton Park.

MORAL.

Now let me add a moral, ere I finish up my lay,
It isn't safe to buy a brush, and hook it off away ;
But, if you will—let me advise each riding, sporting gent
Choose days when B—df—rd isn't out, and when there isn't
   scent.

By The Hon. King Harman.

BILLESDON COPLOW.

" *Quæque ipse miserrima vidi,*
Et quorum pars magna fui."

With the wind at north-east, forbiddingly keen,
The Coplow of Billesdon ne'er witnessed, I ween,
Two hundred such horses and men, at a burst,
All determin'd to ride—each resolv'd to be first.
But to get a good start over eager and jealous,
Two-thirds, at the least, of these very fine fellows,
So crowded, and hustled, and jostled, and cross'd,
That they rode the wrong way, and at starting were lost.
In spite of th' unpromising state of the weather,
Away broke the fox, and the hounds close together :
A burst up to Tilton so brilliantly ran
Was scarce ever seen in the mem'ry of man.
What hounds guided scent, or which led the way,
Your bard—to their names quite a stranger—can't say ;
Tho' their names had he known, he is free to confess,
His horse could not shew him at such a death-pace.

VILLIERS, CHOLMONDELEY, and FORESTER, made such sharp
    play,
Not omitting GERMAINE, never seen till to-day:
Had you judg'd of these four by the trim of their pace,
At Bib'ry you'd thought they'd been riding a race.
But these hounds with a scent—how they dash and they fling,
To o'erride them is quite the impossible thing!
Disdaining to hang in the wood—thro' he raced,
And the open for Skeffington gallantly faced,
Where, headed and foil'd, his first point he forsook,
And merrily led them a dance o'er the brook.
Pass'd Galby, and Norton, Great Stretton and Small,
Right onward still sweeping to old Stretton Hall:
Where two minutes' check served to shew, at one ken,
The extent of the havoc 'mongst horses and men.
Such sighing, such sobbing, such trotting, such walking—
Such reeling, such halting, of fences such baulking—
Such a smoke in the gaps, such comparing of notes—
Such quizzing each other's daub'd breeches and coats:
Here a man walk'd afoot, who his horse had half killed,
There you met with a steed who his rider had spill'd:
In short, such dilemmas, such scrapes, such distress,
One fox ne'er occasioned, the knowing confess.
But, alas! the dilemmas had scarcely began,
On for Wigston and Aylston he resolute ran,
Where a few of the stoutest now slacken'd and panted,
And many were seen irretrievably planted.
The high road to Leicester the scoundrel then cross'd,

As *Tell-Tale*[1] and *Beaufremont*[2] found to their cost ;
And VILLIERS esteem'd it a serious bore
That no longer could *Shuttlecock*[3] fly as before ;
Even *Joe Miller's*[4] spirit of fun was so broke,
That he ceased to consider the run as a joke.
Then streaming away, o'er the river he splash'd—
GERMAINE, close at hand, off the bank, *Melon*[5] dash'd.
Why the *Dun* prov'd so stout, in a scamper so wild,
Till now he had only been rode by a CHILD.[6]
After him plunged *Joe Miller* with MUSTERS so slim,
Who twice sank, and nearly paid dear for his whim,
Not reflecting that all water melons must swim.
Well sous'd by their dip, on they brushed o'er the bottom,
With liquor on board enough to besot 'em ;
But the villain no longer at all at a loss,
Stretch'd away like a devil for Enderby Gorse :
Where meeting with many a brother and cousin,
Who knew how to dance a good hay in the furzen,
JACK RAVEN[7] at length, coming up on a hack,
Which a farmer had lent him—whipp'd off the game pack.
Running sulky, old *Loadstone*[8] the stream would not swim,
No longer sport proving a magnet to him.
   Of mistakes, and mishaps, and what each man befel,
Would the Muse could with justice poetical tell !
BOB GROSVENOR on *Plush*[9]—tho' determin'd to ride—
Lost, at first, a good start, and was soon set aside,
Tho' he charg'd hill and dale, not to lose this rare chase.
On Velvet—*Plush* could not get footing, alas!

To Tilton sail'd bravely Sir WHEELER O'CUFF,
Where neglecting, thro' hurry, to keep a good luff,
To leeward he drifts—how provoking a case !
And was forc'd, tho' reluctant, to give up the chase.

As making his way to the pack's not his forte,
Sir LAWLEY [10] as usual, lost half of the sport,
But then the profess'd philosophical creed,
That—" all's for the best " of Master CANDIDE,
If not comfort Sir R. reconcile may at least ;
For, on *this* supposition, *his* sport is the best.

ORBY HUNTER, who seem'd to be hunting his fate,
Got falls to the tune of no fewer than eight.
Basan's King [11] upon *Glimpse,* [12] sadly out of condition,
Pull'd up, to avoid being tir'd the suspicion.
He did right ; for OG very soon found
His worst had he done, he'd have scarce glimps'd a hound.

CHARLES MEYNELL, who lay very well with the hounds,
Till of Stretton he nearly arriv'd at the bounds,
Now discovered that *Wagoner* [13] rather would creep,
Than exert his great prowess in taking a leap.
But when crossing the turnpike, he read— " Put on here "
'Twas enough to make any one bluster and swear ;
The *Wagoner* feeling familiar the road,
Was resolv'd not to quit it ; so stock still he stood.
Yet prithee, dear CHARLES ! why rash vows will you make,
Thy leave of old Billesdon [14] to finally take ?
Since from Segg's Hill [15] for instance, or perhaps Melton Spinney,
If they go a good pace, you are beat for a guinea !

'Tis money, they say, makes the mare to go kind :
The proverb has vouch'd for this time out of mind.
But tho' of this truth you admit the full force,
It may not hold so good of every horse.
If it did, ELLIS CHARLES need not hustle and hug,
By name, not by nature, his favourite *Slug*.[16]
Yet Slug as he is—the whole of this chase,
CHARLES ne'er could have seen, had he gone a snail's pace.

Old *Gradus*[17] whose fretting and fuming, at first,
Disqualifies strangely for such a tight burst,
Ere to Tilton arriv'd ceased to pull and to crave,
And tho' fresh*ish* at Stretton, he stepp'd a *pas grave!*
Where, in turning him over a cramp kind of place,
He overturn'd GEORGE, whom he threw on his face :
And on foot to walk home it had sure been his fate,
But that soon he was caught, and tied up to a gate.

Near Wigston occurr'd a most singular joke,
Captain MILLER averr'd that his leg he had broke,—
And bemoan'd, in most piteous expressions, how hard,
By so cruel a fracture, to have his sport marr'd.
In quizzing his friends, he felt little remorse
To finesse the complete doing up of his horse.
Had he told a long story of losing a shoe,
Or of laming his horse, he very well knew
That the Leicestershire Creed, out this truism worms,
" Lost shoes and dead beat are synonymous terms."[18]
So a horse must here learn, whatever he does—
To die game—as at Tyburn—and " die in his shoes."

BETHEL, COX, and TOM SMITH, Messieurs BENNET and
    HAWKE,
Their nags all contriv'd to reduce to a walk.
    MAYNARD's Lord, who detests competition and strife,
As well in the chase as in social life,
Than whom nobody harder has rode in his time,
But to crane[19] now and then, now thinks it no crime—
That he beat some crack riders most fairly may crow,
For he liv'd to the end, tho' he scarcely knows how!
With snaffle and martingale kept in the rear,
His horse's mouth open half up to his ear,
Mr. WARDLE, who threat'ned great things over night,[20]
Beyond Stretton was left in most terrible plight;
Too lean to be press'd yet egg'd on by compulsion,
No wonder his nag tumbled into convulsion.
Ah! had he but lost a fore shoe, or fell lame,
'Twould only his sport have curtail'd, not his fame![21]
LORRAINE,[22] than whom no one his game plays more safe,
Who the last than the first prefers seeing by half—
What with nicking,[23] and keeping a constant look out,
Every turn of the scent surely turn'd to account.
The wonderful pluck of his horse surpris'd some,
But he knew they were making point blank for his home,
" Short home " to be brought we all should desire,
Could we manage the trick like the Enderby Squire.[24]
    WILD SHELLEY[25] at starting, all ears and all eyes,
Who to get a good start all experiments tries.
Yet contriv'd it so ill as to throw out poor Gipsy,[26]

Whom he rattled along as if he'd been tipsy,
To catch them again ; but tho' famous for speed,
She never could touch[27] them, much less get a lead.[28]
So dishearten'd,[29] disjointed, and beat, home he swings,
Not much unlike a fiddler hung upon strings.
An H. H.[30] who in Leicestershire never had been,
So of course such a tickler ne'er could[31] have seen,
Just to see them throw off on a raw[32] horse was mounted,
Who a hound had ne'er seen, or a fence had confronted.
But they found in such style,[33] and went off at such score,[34]
That he could not resist the attempt to see more :
So with scrambling,[35] and dashing,[36] and one rattling fall,[37]
He saw all the fun, up to Stretton's white Hall.
There they anchored—in plight not a little distressing—
The horse being raw, he of course got a dressing !
That wonderful mare of VANNECK's, who till now,
By no chance ever tir'd[38] was taken in tow :
And what's worse, she gave VAN such a devilish jog
In the face with her head, plunging out of a bog,
That with eye black as ink, or as EDWARD's fam'd PRINCE,
Half blind has he been, and quite deaf ever since.
" But let not that mortify thee, Shackaback "—[39]
She only was blown,[40] and came a rare hack !

There CRAVEN too stopp'd—whose misfortune, not fault,
His mare unaccountably vex'd with string halt.[41]
And when she had ceas'd thus spasmodic to prance,
Her mouth 'gan to twitch with St. Vitus's dance.[41]

But how shall describ'd be the fate of ROSE PRICE ?[42]

Whose fav'rite white gelding convey'd him so nice
Thro' thick and thro' thin, that he vow'd and protested,[43]
No money should part them, as long as life lasted.
But the pace[44] that effected, which money could not :
For to part—and in death ! was their no distant lot.
In a fatal blind ditch Carlo Khan's[45] powers fail'd,
Where no lancet[16] nor laudanum[16] either avail'd,
More care[17] of a horse than he took could take no man—
He'd more straw than would serve any lying-in woman.
Still he died ! yet just how, as nobody knows,
It may truly be said—He died " under the Rose."
At the death of poor Khan, Melton[18] feels such remorse,
That they've christen'd that ditch 'the Vale of White horse.'
   Thus ended a chase, which, for distance and speed,
It's fellow we never heard of, or read.
Every species of ground ev'ry horse does not suit,
What's a good Country Hunter[49] may here prove a brute,
And unless for all sorts of strange fences prepar'd,
A man and his horse are sure to be scar'd.
This variety gives constant life to the chase ;
But as FORESTER says[50]—" Sir, what *kills*, is the *pace*."
In most other countries they boast of their breed,
For carrying at times, such a beautiful head ;[51]
But these hounds to carry a head cannot fail,
And constantly too—for by George there's—no tail.[52]
Talk of horses, and hounds, and the system of kennel—
Give me Leicestershire nags—and the hounds of OLD
     MEYNELL.   *By the Rev. Robert Lowth.*

BILLESDON COPLOW SONG,

1800.

Air, " *Derry Down.*"

Was there ever such work, as our leaders oft say,
  Was there ever yet seen such a glorious day!
Not *Meynell* himself, the king of all men,
  Ever saw such a chase, or will ever again.

'Twas at BILLESDON COPLOW, the contest began,
  And away from the covert *Old Reynard* soon ran;
Two hours and a quarter, I think was the time,
  It was beautiful, great, nay indeed 'twas sublime.

At Skeffington Earths, first the villain did try,
  Then making all speed to Tilton did fly;
By Skeffington town he soon after came back,
  And at Tugby was near being caught by the pack.

Then passing to Stretton to Wigston he went,
 And at Aylestone we thought that the rogue must be spent,
But for crossng the river he found a good place,
 And changing at Enderby finish'd the chase.

Scotch, Welsh, Irish, and English together set out,
 Each thinking his horse than his neighbour's more stout ;
You must judge by the nags that were up at the end,
 What riders to quiz and what to commend.

Lorraine and *Lord Maynard* were there, and can tell
 Who in justice's scale hold the balance so well ;
As very good judges and justices too,
 The state of each horse, and what each could do.

But if any one thinks he is quizzed in the song,
 And fancies his case stated legally wrong ;
To Enderby Hall let him go and complain,
 But he'll not mend his case, if he meets with *Lorraine.*

Germaine, the most gallant was first at the river,
Like a spaniel dash'd in, how he made our hearts quiver !
And bold as a lion gave Melon[1] a pull,
Who bent to the stream like Europa's famed Bull.

Jack Musters t' obtain a good place in this song,
 Close on the Dun's heels he soused in headlong ;
Holding fast by the tail, like the rudder of a boat,
 But you'll own *Master Jacky* you wetted your coat.

Close stood on the brink and would fain have gone after,
    But hydrophobia made *Coz* turn at the water :
So he scrambled away as fast as he could,
    And came up with the hounds in Enderby Wood.

I need not say much of *Morpeth* or *Shelley*,
    They called on *Jack* (Skeffington) I suppose for a jelly ;
It's true they ride hard, and swear they are keen,
    But yet in this run they never were seen.

As *Jossy Pontoozle* who says in a burst,
    He finds it quite easy to ride *first and first* ;
Were the chase on the pike, he drawn in a gig,
    I'd then bet three-half-pence on little pound pig.

He defies here all quizzing, and would you know why,
    Why he says as whilst leading he knock'd out an eye :
'Bout a clow and a bough and 'bout brandy he'll bore you ;
    But indeed little Jos makes a mighty rum story,
And you'll see both his eyes if you look straight before you.

For he crawl'd to a cot when first he grew blunt,
    Lest his mare should take staggers, vertigo, and grunt ;
Where pig in a pound and snug as you please,
    He was found laying siege to an old woman's cheese.

What became of *Bob Grosvenor* no poet can tell,
    For not long with the hounds did the gay bishop dwell ;
He met brother *Louth*, and 'tis said by the people,
    These parsons climbed up upon Skeffington steeple.

Here they sat quite content like parson and clerk,
    And talk'd o'er the thing till pretty near dark ;
Then the Bishop began to take fright at the weather,
    And their nags being freshen'd went to Melton together.

As 'twas late in the day, the gallant *Lord Craven*,
    Finding matters grew serious kept close to *Jack Raven* ;[3]
But the old raven croak'd when his horse was near done,
    So he changed with a farmer and finished the run.

In this state of distress my Lord—*Maddocks* saw,
    Who just then in his horse had discover'd a flaw ;
Together they join'd, and took leave of the pack,
    Maddocks stumped home on foot, but the peer got a hack.

Of *Patrick Montgomery* and *Wheeler O' Cuff*,
    By jove ! who swear they ride nought but what's tough ;
Sure the plan is not bad, but this day held not good,
    For the couple were nigh being stopp'd by the mud.

Now the straightest way home going round by the bogs,
    Talking o'er this cursed Union, and *Meynell's* swift dogs ;
They trudged home together, still cursing the mud,
    In their minds right resolving to shoot their whole stud.

Charles Meynell got in, but none knows from where,
    For had Old Nick appeared he could not more stare ;
We heard that the wagon was passing the road,
    But why did not Wagoner[4] stop with his load.

Of a mighty great king how it lowers his pride,
　　To be walking on foot when his subjects did ride ;
They in numbers pass'd by, to no one he spoke,
　　But like Charley the Second got up in an Oak.

Fresh from Holland returned, full of water and gin,
　　In Dutch Brogues, *Mynheer Cholmondeley* could not scuffle in;
But riding the cumbrance to cool his hot blood,
　　Served as napkin for *Wardle*, lay snug in the mud.

Tho' late in my song, yet perish the thought,
　　That gallant *Lord Villiers* should e'er be forgot;
Some disaster, I fancy, his lordship befel,
　　For a more dashing rider ne'er gallop'd like ——.

Lord Charles rode on Marquis, so famed for his blood,
　　And shared all the dangers, except in the flood :
Charles Ellis came up too, upon a fresh horse,
　　So we saw by the change that he was not the worse.

I had almost forgot friend *Lawley's* gay Robert,
　　Who, like *Pig*, had an eye to the old woman's cupboard ;
" Horse fresh as a rose," ne'er carried more steady,
　　Only just canter'd home as dinner was ready.

How we lost *Muckle Miller* on Benton's brown Barber,
　　'Tis cruel indeed a conjecture to harbour ;
But we only just heard he could " no stir a peg,"
　　And swore by " St. Saunders" he'd broken his leg.

Tom Smith in the contest maintained a good place,
    And tho' not in first, made a famous good race ;
I'm sure he's no cause his horse to abuse,
    Yet I wish he'd persuade him to keep on his shoes.

At length *Saville* came up, all funking and fears,
    His heart having beat at each fence 'gainst his ears ;
His nag's flank beat high too, which he said was fire,
    For 'tis death to allow, that his tits can e'er tire.

I think I've now bor'd you enough with the chase,
    But like *Meynell's hounds*, I've run a good pace ;
Then a bumper my boys to old *Meynell* let's fill,
    And to those that ride hard, may they never stand still.

                                        Anonymous.

COTTESMORE HUNTING SONG.

"HARK! HARK! JOLLY SPORTSMEN."

Hark! hark! jolly sportsmen, awhile to my tale,
Which to gain your attention, I'm sure will not fail;
Of Lads, and of Horses, of days that ne'er tire,
O'er hedges, and ditches, thro' dale, bog, and mire;—
There's a pack of such Hounds, and a set of such Men,
It's a hundred to-one if we meet with again—
Had Nimrod that mightiest of hunters been there,
By Jove,—he'd have shook like an Aspen for fear!

Fal, lal, &c.

In seventeen hundred and seventy one,
The 5th of November, or 6th—it's all one,
At eight in the morning, by most of the clocks,
We rode off from Cottesmore in search of a Fox:
There was Exton Town Landlord, and bold Horace Mann,
Long Powis, Old Sussex, and Sly Sylivan;
Parson Lambert, Tom Noel, those hunters so stout,
Sam, Charles, a few others, and so we set out!

Fal, lal, &c.

We cast off our hounds for an hour or more,
When Crowner sets up a most terrible roar,
"Hark to Crowner," cries Will, and the rest were not slack,
For Crowner's no trifler esteem'd in the pack :
There's Bluster, and Nancy, comes readily in,
And the rest of the hounds join'd the musical din ;
Had Diana been there, she'd been pleased to the life,
For bold Horace Mann had a Goddess to Wife !

Fal, lal, &c.

Few minutes past ten was the time of the day,
When Reynard broke cover, and this was his way :
He sprung from great Owston as tho' he'd no fear,
Thro' Launde Wood and Tilton, his course he did steer :
Thro' Loddington Reddish, and then right across,
Up Buttermilk Hill, and Stapleford Gorse ;
At Round Story's, he brushed Lord Harboro's Wall,
And seem'd to say "little I value you all !"

Fal, lal, &c.

To Leesthorpe he ran, and thro' Suffill's deep grounds,
Dick Branston, Tom Church, at the tail of the hounds,
The earths they were open, but he was too stout,
He might have gone in, but he choose to keep out ;—
Over Whissendine Brook was the way that he flew,
At Ranksborough Cover we had him in view,
He drove on at Rocott, at Branston he waded,
Prior's Coppice he travers'd, poor Suffill got jaded !

Fal, lal, &c.

Thro' O'erton-Park-Wood, like an arrow he passed,
Drove back by the steep hills of Burley at last,—
He gallantly threw himself into the garden,
" Barlowly " he cries, " I don't heed ye a farthing."—
But soon he perceived that there were no bounds
Could stop the pursuit of such staunch mettled hounds;
His policy did not serve him a rush,
Five couple of Tartars were close at his brush!

Fal, lal, &c.

To recover the Park then again was his play,
But as thro' the pales he could not make his way,
He found he of speed and of cunning grew slack,
Then was way-laid and kill'd by the rest of the pack ;—
At his death there were present the lads I have sung,
Indeed Kitty Fisher, and Suffill got flung,—
Thus ended at length this heart-stirring chase,
Which lasted five hours and ten minutes' pace !

Fal, lal, &c.

We return'd to Peer Gainsborough's plentiful board,
Where dwells hospitality, truth, and my lord ;
We talked o'er the chase, and toasted a health,
"To all Fox Hunting Squires at the places of wealth !"
Horace Mann bilked a leap,—said Long Powis it's odd,
Cries Lambert he sinn'd by Diana's bright rod ;
Says Stevens,—" I halloo'd get up tho' you fall,
Or I'll leap over you, your bald gelding and all!"

Fal, lal, &c.

Each glass was adapted to freedom and sport,
For party affairs were consigned to the court,
Thus finish'd the rest of the day, and the night,
In gay flowing bumpers, and social delight ;—
Then early next morn, bade farewell to each brother,
Some they went one way, and some went another ;
As Phœbus befriended us early at morn,
So Luna took care in conducting us home !

        Fal, lal, &c.

         Anonymous.

THE HIGH-METTLED RACER.

See the course throng'd with gazers,—the sports are begun ;
The confusion but hear !—' I'll bet you, sir,'—' Done, done :'
Ten thousand strange murmurs resound far and near ;
Lords, hawkers, and jockeys, assail the tir'd ear ;—
While with neck like a rainbow, erecting his crest,
Pamper'd, prancing, and pleas'd, his head touching his breast,
Scarcely snuffing the air, he's so proud and elate,
The high-mettled racer first starts for the plate.

Now Reynard's turn'd out : and o'er hedge and ditch rush
Hounds, horses, and huntsmen, all hard at his brush ;
They run him at length, and they have him at bay,
And by scent and by view cheat a long tedious way ;
While, alike born for sports of the field and the course,
Always sure to come through, a staunch and fleet horse,
When fairly run down, the fox yields up his breath,
The high-mettled racer is in at the death.

Grown aged, us'd up, and turn'd out of the stud,
Lame, spavin'd, and wind-gall'd, but yet with some blood,
While knowing postillions his pedigree trace,
Tell his dam won this sweepstakes, his sire gain'd that race,
And what matches he won, too, the hostlers count o'er,
As they loiter their time at some hedge-alehouse door ;
While the harness sore galls, and the spurs his sides goad,
The high-mettled racer's a hack on the road.

Till at last, having labour'd, drudg'd early and late,
Bow'd down by degrees, he bends on to his fate ;
Blind, old, lean, and feeble, he tugs round a mill,
Or draws sand, till the sand of his hourglass stands still ;
And now, cold and lifeless, expos'd to the view,
In the very same cart which he yesterday drew,
While a pitying crowd his sad relics surrounds,
The high-mettled racer is sold for the hounds.

By Charles Dibdin.

THE WILY FOX.

The morning breaks;
Those ruddy streaks
Proclaim the op'ning day;
With glowing health,
The sportsman's wealth;—
Away, boys, come away.
The mellow horn
On the still morn
Pours sounds which echo mocks,
While following bound
Man, horse, and hound,
T' unearth the wily fox.
Hark! echo mocks
The winding horn,
That on th' expanded wing of morn,
Though sweet the sound, in dreadful yell
Tolls out a knell
To the devoted fox.

Now off he's thrown,
　The day's our own,—
See yonder where he takes;
　To cheat our eyes,
　In vain he tries
The rivers and the brakes.
　The mellow horn
　Breaks on the morn,
And leads o'er hills and rocks;
　While following bound
　Man, horse, and hound,
To o'ertake the wily fox.
　　　　　Hark! echo mocks, &c.

Now, now he's seiz'd!
　The hounds, well pleas'd
Behold his eye-balls roll :
　He yields his breath,
　And from his death
Is born the flowing bowl.
　The mellow horn,
　That through the morn
Led over hills and rocks,
　Now sounds a call,
　To see the fall
Of the expiring fox.
　　　　　Hark! echo mocks, &c.

　　　　　By Charles Dibdin.

H

ECHO.

When from the glowing blush of morn
  The sober night's retreating,
And jocund nature, newly born,
  Her children all are greeting,
Ten thousand sounds on ether float,
And ev'ry being's grateful note
Awakens Echo, blithe, Echo, blithe Echo.
                     And ev'ry, &c.

But loudest sound the hunting crew
  When horn and hound are vieing,
And man and horse, the game in view,
  O'er hedge and ditch are flying ;
Then to exhilirate the pack,
Each jocund accent is sent back,
By merry Echo, blithe Echo, blithe Echo.
                     Each jocund, &c.

The love-struck shepherd seeks her cave,
  When Celia bids him languish,

And fears that nothing but the grave
  Can ease his hopeless anguish :
He vainly for relief may call ;
He finds his expectations all
An empty Echo, mere Echo, sad Echo.

                    He finds, &c.

Not so the sturdy woodman's sound,
  When oaks and elms he's felling,
The forest's pride extended round,
  To rear some lordly dwelling :
While at each stroke his hatchet rings,
In ev'ry cheerful note he sings,
Joins merry Echo, sweet Echo, blithe Echo.

                    In ev'ry, &c.

The miser, would he hide his store,
  Seeks out for close recesses,
Lest any should that hoard explore,
  Withheld from man's distresses :
Himself, still needing most relief,
Fears ev'ry breeze, and dreads a thief
In murm'ring Echo, sad Echo, vex'd Echo.

                    Fears ev'ry, &c.

Not so gay Bacchus' laughing train,
  Of joy that fill the measure,
That sport the jest, and troll the strain,
  And know no end of pleasure :

They, dull advice and care asleep,
Rouse, as their merry rites they keep,
The jolly Echo, sweet Echo, blithe Echo.

                    Rouse as, &c.

Our actions Echo, then reflects,
    As mirrors show our faces ;
Which, broken, multiply defects,
    As well as charms and graces.
On all who are to honour blind,
The execrations of mankind
Shall tire the Echo, harsh Echo, shrill Echo.

                    The execrations, &c.

But ye, who, friends to social mirth
    And rational enjoyment,
Seek out and nurture private worth,
    Pursue your sweet employment :
Go on,—of truth redress the wrongs,
Till blessings from a thousand tongues
Shall sweetly Echo, bless'd Echo, sweet Echo.

                    Till blessings, &c.

                    By Charles Dibdin.

TANTIVY.

Let sons of sloth dream time away,
 Regardless what may follow,
And rail at us who wake the day
 With horn, and hound, and halloo :
We their pursuits should find the same,
 To their secrets were we privy;
Each man to hunt some fav'rite game
 Through life goes on tantivy.

The book-worm hunts the ancient schools,
 And walks with Aristotle ;
Black-legs and ladies hunt for fools ;
 The toper hunts his bottle.
Thus should we find, whate'er the name,
 To their secrets were we privy,
             Mankind to hunt, &c.

When doctors come in at the death—
 For true-bred hunters these are—

The patient cries, with his last breath,
  '*Et tu, Brute!*—then fall Cæsar.'
Thus we with safety might proclaim,
  To their secrets were we privy,
                Mankind to hunt, &c.

The misanthrope hunts out for woes ;
  Muck-worms are gold pursuing ;
While neck-or-nothing, as he goes,
  The spendthrift hunts his ruin.
               Thus, &c.

Bold tars for honour hunt the wind ;
  Outrageous saints hunt sinners ;
While with round belly, capon-lin'd,
  Fat Aldermen hunt dinners.
Thus should we find men's views the same,
  To their secrets were we privy,
              All, all to hunt, &c.

Fame courtiers hunt from place to place ;
  Rakes hunt new sets and features ;
While gen'rous hearts urge on the chase,
  To relieve their fellow-creatures :
Let us, while to our actions' aim
  Regardless who are privy,
In chase of pleasure, as fair game,
  Though life go on tantivy.

               By Charles Dibdin.

THE MELLOW TON'D HORN.

The gray-eye'd Aurora, in saffron array,
   'Twixt my curtains in vain took a peep,
And though broader and broader still brighten'd the day,
   Naught could wake me, so sound did I sleep.
At length rosy Phœbus look'd full in my face,
   Full and fervent; but nothing would do,
Till the hounds yelp'd, impatient, and long'd for the chase,
   And shouting appear'd the whole crew.
Come on; yoics, honies! hark! forward, my boys,
   There ne'er was so charming a morn;
Follow, follow; wake Echo, to share in our joys—
   Now the music, now echo—mark! mark!
   Hark! hark!
The silver-mouth'd hounds, and the mellow-ton'd horn.

Fresh as that smiling morning from which they draw health,
   My companions are rang'd on the plain,
Bless'd with rosy contentment, that nature's best wealth,
   Which monarchs aspire to in vain;

Now spirits like fire ev'ry bosom invade,
    And now we in order set out,
While each neighbouring valley, rock, woodland, and glade,
    Re-vollies the air-rending shout.

Come on, &c.

Now Renard's unearth'd, and runs fairly in view,—
    Now we've lost him, so subtl'y he turns ;
But the scent lies so strong, still we fearless pursue,
    While each object impatiently burns :
Hark ! Babbler gives tongue, and Fleet, Driver, and Sly ;
    The fox now the covert forsakes ;
Again he's in view, let us after him fly,—
    Now, now to the river he takes.

Come on, &c.

From the river poor Renard can make but one push,
    No longer so proudly he flies ;
Tir'd, jaded, worn out, we are close to his brush,
    And conquer'd, like Cæsar, he dies.
And now in high glee to the board we repair,
    Where sat, as we jovially quaff,
His portion of merit let ev'ry man share,
    And promote the convivial laugh.

Come on, &c.

By Charles Dibdin.

NOTES.

NOTES TO SOUTH STAFFORDSHIRE HUNTING SONG, 1875.

PAGE 9. Note *.

John Perks is a Solicitor
    Of famous Burton town,
And Frederick Gretton is a Swell
    Of Sterling good renown.

Says G. to P. " I've got a grey,
    The very best of cobs, sir ! "
Say P. to G. " I've got a mare
    Will beat him for a bob, sir ! "

" Good ! said F. G., " we'll run a race,
    For fifty pounds, my mon,"
To which the bold Solicitor
    Replied with pluck " You're on ! "

" We'll run it on the Lichfield Course
    Judge Trevor in the box ;
The starter we will both agree
    Shall be the " Wily Fox." "*

The match was made—no sporting match
    Was fairer e'er or truer :—
The point to test was which was best,
    The Lawyer or the Brewer.

Eighteen stone six (a trifling weight)
    The horses had to bear ;
The Brewer on his gallant grey,
    The Lawyer on " T'ould mare."

Then both shook hands, and both did
        swear
    To do their best endeavour
To be the first on Lichfield course
    To catch the eye of Trevor.

Most people thought the Lawyer's 'cause'
    Was one he would be lost in :

They little knew the trainer sly
    He'd got in Tommy Austin.

When the day came, " T'ould mare "
        arrived
    With Frederick's gallant grey :
And when the wily fox said " Go ! "
    Both tried to get away.

Alas ! " T'ould mare " she would not
        move ;
While Frederick, with a smile,
Sprung to the fore, and gained at least
    A quarter of a mile.

The Lawyer thought his " case was
        quashed,"
    And his " conveyance " bad ;—
But, putting " wills " and " deeds "
        aside,
    Went after Fred like mad.

Said Gretton, " I will not beat
    By any quips or quirks ! "
But the stern law was after him,
    In shape of Lawyer Perks.

Frederick fermented in his casque
    (That day 'twas painted blue,)
When Lawyer Perks arrested him,
    And tried his cause to sue.

They rush ! They rush ! 'mid deafening
        cheers,
    They test their horses' strength,
Till cheers from the Grand Stand an-
        nounce
    " The Baron, by a length ! "

*The Author of this Book.
N.B.—These spirited lines are from the pen of a distinguished scholar well known
at Burton, and a great friend of Mr. Perks's.

PAGE 12.

Note †. Mr. John Bamford, of Glas-
cote, as fine a rider as ever went out.

PAGE 14,

Note ‡. Huntsman to Lord Anson
and Mr. Applethwaite with the Atherstone.

——:o:——

NOTES TO BILLESDON COPLOW.

PAGE 42.

Note 1. Mr. Forester's horse.

Note 2. Mr. Maddock's horse.

Note 3. Lord Villiers's horse.

Note 4. Mr. Musters's horse.

Note 5. Mr. Germaine's horse.

Note 6. Formerly the property of Mr.
Child, to whom this hunt is perhaps
originally indebted for the present spirited style of riding to hounds.

Note 7. The name of the huntsman.

Note 8. The huntsman's horse.

Note 9. Mr. Robert Grosvenor's horse.

PAGE 43.

Note 10. Sir Robert Lawley—not unusually in the brief dialect of Melton
called Sir Lawley.

Note 11. Mr. Oglander; who according to the same dialect goes by the more
familiar appellation of Og.

Note 12. Mr. Oglander's horse.

Note 13. Mr. Charles Meynell's horse.

Note 14. He had threatened again
never to attempt following the hounds
from Billesdon, as no horse could carry
his weight up to them in that part of the
country.

Note 15. A very different part of the
hunt.

PAGE 44.

Note 16. Mr. Charles Ellis's horse.

Note 17. Mr. George Ellis's horse.

Note 18. Indeed so implicit is this
article of the Meltonian belief, that many
a horse in addition to the misfortune of
break in his hoof from losing his shoe,
has laboured likewise under the aforesaid
unavoidable imputation, to his everlast-
ing disgrace!

PAGE 45.

Note 19. The term derives its origin
from the necessary extension of neck of
such sportsmen as dare to incur the
reproach by venturing "to look before they leap."

Note 20. Who was said to have threatened, that he would beat the whole field
the next day.

Note 21. For which express purpose,
more than *sport*, some are *silly* enough to
suppose he hunts; and which, though he
did actually succeed in, in *one* instance
some seasons ago, he probably never will
do again, having threatened it frequently since with as little success.

Note 22. Mr Lorraine Smith.

Note 23. A term of great reproach,
according to the above dialect, to those
who are so shabby as to cut across to the
hounds, when it is esteemed so much
more honorable to follow their very
track; by which spirited line of conduct
they may be pretty certain of never seeing them at all!

PAGE 45.

Note 24. Where Mr. Lorraine Smith lives.

Note 25. Sir John Shelley: wild with joy must be here meant; as no one can be personally more serious and sedate: indeed, if the worthy Baronet has a foible it is gravity.

Note 26. Sir John Shelley's mare.

PAGE 46.

Note 27. According to the Melton dialect, *overtake*.

Note 28. By which is to be understood, securing the privilege of breaking your neck first; and when you fall, of being rode over by a hundred and ninety-nine of the best fellows upon earth to a dead certainty.

Note 29. Nor can that astonish any one when it is considered what an inestimable privilege he has lost.

Note 30. It is not quite clear whether these initials are meant to apply to a Hampshire hog, or the Hampshire hunt. If to the hog, it does not appear that he saved his bacon.

Note 31. *(Meltonice)* a run so severe, that there is no laughing at it.

Note 32. *(Meltonice)* a horse who knew nothing of the business he was going about, or wished to know.

Note 33. *Style* means the best possible manner of doing any thing. As for instance, when a man rides his horse full speed at double posts, and rails, with a *Squire Trap* on the the other side, (which is a moderate ditch of about two yards wide, cut on purpose to break gentlemen's necks), he is then reckoned, at Melton, to have rode it in style; especially if he is caught in the said Squire Trap.

Note 34. That kind of pace which perhaps neither you nor your horse ever went before; and if you have not more luck than falls to the share of every first experiment of the kind 'tis ten to one but he falls before he can (what they call) get on his legs; in which case you may rest perfectly satisfied that he must roll over you two or three times at least before he can stop himself.

PAGE 46.

Note 35. When a horse does not leave above three of his legs behind him, and saves himself by pitching on his head!

Note 36. When a man *charges* a fence (which no other word can express so fully) on the other side of which it is impossible to guess what mischief awaits him, but where his getting a fall is reduced as nearly as possible to a moral certainty.

Note 37. Rattling fall: Q.E.D.

Note 38. Which, if other proof were wanting, ascertains beyond anything else the severity of this chase.

Note 39. A familiar appellation, borrowed from Blue Beard, and bestowed by his friends at Melton on Mr. Vanneck, than which nothing can more thoroughly prove the estimation in which his society is held there; since none but good fellows are ever esteemed, according to the Meltonian principles, worthy of a nick name.

Note 40. His own observation, the merit of which I would scorn to assume; but for the truth of which (at least the latter assertion) I can vouch, as I perfectly agree with him, that I never saw a more complete hack, though he is pleased to call her a hunter.

Note 41. Two nervous affections, in every sense of the word very distressing, especially to a by-stander, who cannot command his risible muscles upon so melancholy an occasion.

Note 42. A gentleman, of whom it has been erroneously said that he never returned from hunting but his horse was sure to be either lame or knocked up.

PAGE 47.

Note 43. At the covert side his horse had been particularly admired, and a considerable sum of money offered for him.

Note 44. A complete answer to that impertinent question so vauntingly asked by a favourite poet, when he exclaims, in language indeed somewhat bold, "Pray what can do that which money can not?"

Note 45. The name of Mr Price's horse.

PAGE 17.

Note 46. Two excellent restoratives where the patient is not too far gone.

Note 47. Indeed it is only to be lamented, that Mr. P. had not taken rather more care of him a little earlier in the day, which probably would have obviated the necessity of this *accouchement*.

Note 48. Which redounds highly to the credit and the sympathy of the Melton gentlemen, and completely refutes a very ill-natured but groundless supposition, that their sensibility will ever suffer them to make a joke of any such heavy loss a gentleman may happen to sustain, especially if the gentleman likewise happens to be heavy himself, which of course, doubles the weight of the misfortune.

Note 49. As every *Country* Gentleman may not understand the force of this expression, he ought to know, that the Meltonians hold every horse that cannot "*Go along at a slapping pace*," "*Stay at that pace*," "*Skim ridge and furrow*," "*Catch his horses*," "*Top a flight of rails*," "*Come well in the next field*," "*Charge an ox fence*," "*Go in and out clever*," "*Face a Brush*," "*Swish at a rasper*," and in short, "*Do all that kind of thing*," phrases so plain and intelligible, that it is impossible

PAGE 47.

to mistake their meaning! A horse is held in the same contempt in Leicestershire, as a coxcomb holds a country bumpkin. In vulgar countries (*i.e.* all others) where these accomplishments are not indispensable he may be a hunter.

Note 50. A gentleman who practically explains all the above accomplishments to the great edification of young horses, and the no less astonishment of weak minds!

Note 51. A favourite maxim of Mr. Forester's, of the truth of which he seldom loses an opportunity of endeavouring to make his friends thoroughly sensible.

Note 52. As heads and tails are not here to be understood in the common acceptation of the words, and as all ladies are not sportswomen enough to be aware that they have no reference to the human head or tail, they should know, that when you can "cover the hounds with a sheet" (which any Meltonian will explain to them more particularly) they are then said to carry a beautiful head; when on the contrary, they follow the leader in a line, like a flight of wild fowls, they are then said to tail.

—:0:—

NOTES TO BILLESDON COPLOW SONG, 1800.

PAGE 49.

Note 1. The name of a horse.

PAGE 50.

Note 2. Mr. Cox, a Gentleman of Northampton, with only one arm, who appears in the original painting, and no other.

PAGE 51.

Note 3. The Huntsman.

Note 4. The name of the horse.

EGGINGTON AND BROWN, LICHFIELD.

.

www.ingramcontent.com/pod-product-compliance
Lightning Source LLC
Chambersburg PA
CBHW021427090426
42742CB00009B/1287